CCSS Genre Expository Text

P9-DHT-699

? Essential Question
How do teams work together?

Firefighting Heroes

by Kate Sinclair

Introduction 2

Chapter 1
United We Stand 4

Chapter 2
Firefighters at Work 8

Chapter 3
Safety in the Home 12

Conclusion 14

Respond to Reading 15

PAIRED READ A Favor Repaid 16

Glossary/Index 19

Focus on Social Studies 20

Introduction

Long ago, people needed fire to survive. They used fire to cook and to keep warm, but accidental fire was always a danger. Buildings in many early settlements were made of wood. These small settlements were often surrounded by forest. There was no running water that people could use to put out the fires, and there were no fire departments to call. A fire could destroy an entire village in just moments!

The Great Fire of London destroyed more than 13,000 houses and 400 streets, as well as hundreds of churches, schools, and other public buildings.

In 1666, a terrible fire—now known as the Great Fire of London—swept through the streets of London for just over three days. Thousands of homes were destroyed, and many people died.

The scary thing about this fire was that it started in one small shop. The city had narrow streets and wood houses that were close together. The fire started on a windy day. The wind helped to push the fire quickly across the city.

Big disasters like the Great Fire made people realize that they needed to band together to protect themselves from fire.

Heritage Images/CORBIS

CHAPTER 1

United We Stand

Fire was a problem for the first settlers in America. Settlers from England arrived in Jamestown, Virginia, in 1607. In the first year of the settlement, a fire nearly destroyed the whole **colony**. Almost all of the houses were burned to the ground.

It was not only Jamestown that suffered from harmful fires in the seventeenth century. There were two big fires in Boston in 1653 and 1676.

People realized that they needed to respond quickly to fires. The **colonists** began to form **volunteer** firefighting teams. Their purpose was to fight fires as well as to prevent fires from starting in the first place.

Fighting Fire in the 1600s

It took many volunteers to put out fires. People put buckets of water outside of their houses each night. If a fire broke out, volunteers would race from home to home collecting the buckets. They would use a long pole to pick up and carry the buckets. Then the volunteers would race to the fire with the water.

Fire damaged many buildings in American cities. This building, which housed a New York newspaper, was destroyed in 1882.

The city of Philadelphia was **founded** by William Penn in 1682. Penn had witnessed the Great Fire of London. He tried to prevent fire when planning his new city. He designed wide streets and kept open areas of land so that it would be difficult for fire to spread over large areas. People were ordered to clean their chimneys regularly. Many new buildings were built from brick rather than from wood.

This is the first fire engine ever built in the United States.

(t) Museum of the City of New York/Corbis, (b) Bettmann/CORBIS

Benjamin Franklin was one of our founding fathers. He started a volunteer firefighting group in Philadelphia. Franklin had witnessed fires in Boston, where he grew up, so he understood the dangers of fire.

In 1736, Franklin started a fire brigade called The Union Fire Company. It had 30 volunteers. These volunteers were heroes in their community. It was not long before other fire companies sprang up around Philadelphia.

Franklin modeled his fire company after the ones he had seen in Boston.

Women Firefighters

Women began volunteering in the early 1800s. The first known female firefighter was an African American woman named Molly Williams. Molly fought fires in New York wearing a dress and an apron. Marina Betts was another female volunteer. Marina was well known in Pittsburgh for throwing buckets of water over men who wouldn't help fight fires!

Library of Congress Prints & Photographs Division [LC-USZC2-2004]

Working together as a team was a very important part of being a volunteer firefighter in Benjamin Franklin's time. It took a lot of effort to collect buckets of water from outside people's homes and transport these buckets to the fire.

Volunteers would also create bucket brigades. They would form a line, with one end near the fire and the other near a source of water. Then they would pass the buckets of water down the line from one person to another. This way, they could get water to the fire as quickly as possible.

Today's modern equipment makes fighting fires easier. However, firefighters still need to work together as a team to do this important job.

These firefighters use a special ladder on the fire truck, with a hose attached, to fight a fire in Atlanta, Georgia.

Skip Nall/Photodisc/Getty Images

CHAPTER 2

Firefighters at Work

Today, there are more than 30,000 fire departments in the United States. Almost 90 percent of these fire departments are either completely or partly staffed by volunteers. This amounts to more than 800,000 people! Many of these volunteers work in small, **rural** fire departments. All volunteers have a sense of **civic duty**. They volunteer so that they can protect people and help out in their community.

Today's firefighters use modern equipment, including high-pressure hoses, to fight fires.

Mark Karrass/CORBIS

Firefighters often work with the members of other teams, such as paramedics.

Firefighters work in teams, but there is usually a captain in charge. He or she gives duties to each firefighter. These duties can change at a moment's notice. That means that all firefighters have to learn to drive the fire truck, hook up the hoses, position the ladders, and enter burning buildings safely.

Volunteer firefighters do more than fight fires. Sometimes, they also help out during natural disasters, car accidents, and medical emergencies.

Even when there is not a fire, there is still work to be done around the station. The team needs to wash the fire trucks and take care of all the other equipment.

Mike Watson Images/Alamy

Volunteer firefighters need a lot of training. First, they have to learn about fire safety. They learn to identify different types of fires and how they spread. They learn how to use and maintain all of the fire equipment.

Volunteers also have to pass a physical test as well. They have to be able to crawl through small spaces. They have to be able to drag heavy hoses for several hundred feet and carry them up and down several flights of stairs. Finally, they have to be able to carry a 180-pound dummy through a doorway.

Firefighters must wear protective gear and carry heavy equipment.

Radius/SuperStock

All in a Day's Work

Read about this firefighter's day.

*The alarm is ringing. A house is on fire. We run to the engine. Joe is our driver. We take our seats. My job is to control the hose. Anne looks after the ladders. When we get there, we find that the fire is hard to control. We all have our protective clothing and our breathing **apparatus**. We're not sure if everyone is out of the house. First, we help clear the house. An elderly man is the last person out. He is having trouble breathing. Peter, our first aid officer, gives the man oxygen and helps him to breathe steadily again. We are very pleased that our new equipment helps make sure the fire is out. We are all exhausted! But everyone is safe, and the fire is contained.*

It is important for firefighters to communicate with each other during an emergency.

PBNJ Productions/Blend Images/CORBIS

CHAPTER 3

Safety in the Home

People have been aware of the need for fire prevention and fire safety since the times of early settlements, and it is still very important in our everyday lives. One of a firefighter's jobs is to educate people of all ages about fire safety. Do you know what to do if there is a fire in your home?

Escape!

Think about the layout of your home. What is the safest way out in a fire? Have a family meeting and talk about the best ways out of the house, especially at night. Choose a place away from the house to meet. Choose someone to be in charge of "counting heads," to check that everyone is out. Call the fire department as soon as possible, but never stay in the house to do it.

STOP   **DROP**   **ROLL**

If your clothing catches fire, drop to the floor and roll over to put out the flames.

High-Rise Buildings

If you live in a tall building, know where the nearest fire exit is and make sure you can find your way there in the dark. Remember not to take the elevator during a fire. Never go back inside once you have left the building. Tell the fire department if anyone is still in the building.

Stairs are the safest way out of a high-rise building during a fire.

A working smoke alarm saves lives!

Smoke Alarms

A working smoke alarm can alert you to a fire at any time of the day or night. Homes should have smoke alarms on every level and outside every bedroom. To make sure your smoke alarm is working, the batteries need to be changed every six months. It's a good idea to mark the dates on a calendar as a reminder.

(tr) The McGraw-Hill Companies, Inc./Luke David, photographer, (bl) S. Wanke/PhotoLink/Photodisc/Getty Images

Conclusion

People have known for a long time that it's a good idea to work together to protect the community from fires. Today, many people lead very busy lives. It can be difficult for them to find time to volunteer for services such as firefighting. Yet the work of volunteer firefighters is as important today as it has ever been. Would you consider becoming a volunteer firefighter when you're older?

Firefighters teach people of all ages about fire safety.

DreamPictures/Blend Images LLC

Respond to Reading

Summarize

Use details from *Firefighting Heroes* to summarize the text. Your graphic organizer may help you.

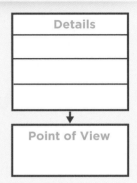

Details

↓

Point of View

Text Evidence

1. How do you know that *Firefighting Heroes* is an expository text? Find two examples of information about firefighters in the text. GENRE

2. How does the author describe volunteer firefighters? Give two examples. AUTHOR'S POINT OF VIEW

3. What do you think *prevent* on page 4 means? What other words in the sentence help you figure out what it means? SENTENCE CLUES

4. Write a paragraph describing how the author feels about volunteer firefighters. WRITE ABOUT READING

Compare Texts
Read about a woman who gets help from a very unusual source.

A Favor Repaid

Sal Fink was the daughter of a famous Mississippi boatman. She was as brave as her father and just as loud. When she yelled, her voice echoed through the entire forest.

One day, Sal was wandering in the forest when she heard grunting from the hollow of a tree. Then she saw three sleeping bear cubs. Sal couldn't help herself —she bent down to pat them. Patting wild animals is not a good idea, but Sal was careless about her safety.

16

Sal heard a low rumble behind her. She turned to face a very angry mother bear. The bear was going to attack, but Sal was equal to the challenge. She yelled, which stopped the bear in its tracks for a moment. Then she wrestled the bear to the ground.

Sal had the bear at her mercy. She looked at the bear, and then she looked at the cubs. She made a decision. She patted the bear and walked away.

A couple of years later, Sal was chopping down a tall tree. She was absorbed in her work and didn't notice that the birds had stopped singing. Suddenly, Sal smelled smoke. When she looked around, she could see flames and hear the crackle of burning wood. Every way Sal looked, she could see flames.

Sal knew how quickly wildfires could spread. She didn't know which way to go to escape. Sal yelled loudly, but there was no one to hear her—or so she thought!

Text: Karen Alexander, Illustration: Helen Tudor

To Sal's amazement, a bear came crashing out of the trees a few minutes later. When Sal bellowed, the bear recognized her voice. The bear feared fire, but it remembered that Sal had spared its life. The bear ran toward Sal and then back the way it had come. Sal realized the bear wanted her to follow.

As Sal ran, she heard trees falling all around her. Eventually, they came to the river. Sal held onto the bear's fur, and it towed her to the other side. Sal clambered out and lay gasping, but safe, on the riverbank. The bear looked at her, made a mumbling sound, and ambled off into the trees. From then on, Sal often caught glimpses of black fur when she was in the forest, but she never saw the bear clearly again.

Text: Karen Alexander, Illustration: Helen Tudor

? Make Connections

How do Sal and the bear work together in *A Favor Repaid*? ESSENTIAL QUESTION

How are *Firefighting Heroes* and *A Favor Repaid* examples of teamwork? TEXT TO TEXT

Glossary

apparatus *(ap-uh-RAT-uhs)* the equipment needed for a particular purpose *(page 11)*

civic duty *(SIV-ik DEW-tee)* the responsibilities of a citizen *(page 8)*

colonists *(KOL-uh-nists)* early settlers *(page 4)*

colony *(KOL-uh-nee)* a place where people first settle in a land that is new to them *(page 4)*

founded *(FOWND-uhd)* started *(page 5)*

rural *(ROOR-uhl)* communities with farms or houses that are far apart *(page 8)*

volunteer *(vol-uhn-TEER)* a person who offers to do a job for no payment *(page 4)*

Index

Boston, *4, 6*

colonists, *4*

equipment, *7–11*

Franklin, Benjamin, *6, 7*

Great Fire of London, *2, 3, 5*

Jamestown, *4*

Penn, William, *5*

Philadelphia, *5, 6*

training, *10*

Focus on Social Studies

Purpose To find out about volunteers.

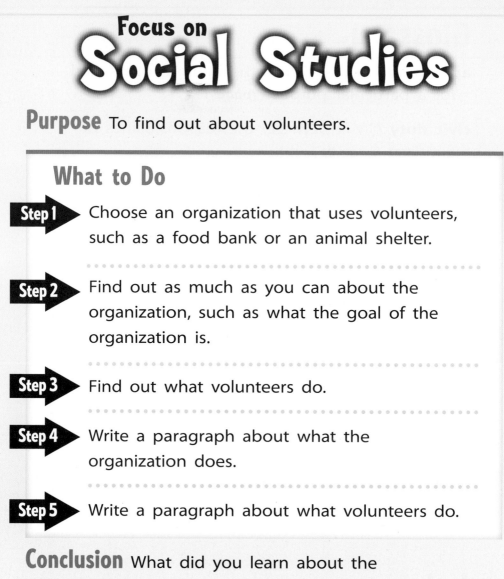

What to Do

Step 1 Choose an organization that uses volunteers, such as a food bank or an animal shelter.

Step 2 Find out as much as you can about the organization, such as what the goal of the organization is.

Step 3 Find out what volunteers do.

Step 4 Write a paragraph about what the organization does.

Step 5 Write a paragraph about what volunteers do.

Conclusion What did you learn about the organization?